Manny's Homework Assignment

by Teresa Vernbow
illustrated by Brandon Reese

SCHOOL PUBLISHERS

D1797540

p.8, ©SuperStock, Inc.; p.10, ©ML Sinibaldi/CORBIS; p.11, ©Gianni Dagli Orti/CORBIS; p.12, ©Schalkwijk/Art Resource, NY; p.13, ©Lindsay Hebberd/CORBIS.

Printed in China

ISBN 10:   0-15-379054-7
ISBN 13:   978-0-15-379054-6

Ordering Options
ISBN 10:   0-15-378787-2 (English Language Development Concept Readers Collection, Grade 4)
ISBN 13:   978-0-15-378787-4 (English Language Development Concept Readers Collection, Grade 4)
ISBN 10:   0-15-379084-9 (package of 5)
ISBN 13:   978-0-15-379084-3 (package of 5)

2 3 4 5 6 7 8 9 10 0940 17 16 15 14 13 12 11 10 09

"Class, I have a very interesting homework assignment for you," said Ms. Richards. "I want you to find out about your cultural heritage."

"What's cultural heritage?" asked Kim.

"It has to do with what country your family first came from," said Ms. Richards. "It's what makes that country special. It's that country's food and holidays. It is music and art. It is language and history."

Manny walked home slowly. He found his mother in her office.

"Mama," he asked. "What is our cultural heritage?"

"That's a big question!" Mama said.

"I need to know for school," said Manny. "What was Mexico like?"

"Oh, my," laughed Mama. "I don't remember. I was born here in the United States, and I grew up in Los Angeles."

"What was that like?" asked Manny.

"It was fun!" said Mama. "There were lots of children in my apartment building. We played together all the time."

"What did you play?" asked Manny.

"Well, we played soccer," said Mama. "My friends and I danced a lot. Also, my best friend's family owned a Mexican restaurant. We spent many hours there."

"That sounds like fun!" said Manny. "Ms. Richards wants us to find out about the country where our family first came from, though."

"Then you should talk to Grandma," said Mama. "She's coming over tonight."

Manny hurried over to talk to Grandma as soon as she walked in the door. "Grandma!" cried Manny. "Please tell me about Mexico!"

"That's some greeting," said Grandma. "Do I get a hug?"

Manny hugged his grandmother. Then he explained the homework assignment. His grandmother nodded as she listened.

"I see," she said. "Mexico has quite a cultural heritage. Where should I start?"

"Where did you grow up?" asked Manny.

"It's wonderful music played with many brass instruments," said Grandma. "Do you remember your Great Uncle Manuel's band that played at Aunt Thalia's wedding?"

"They were great!" said Manny. "Uncle Manuel let me play his trumpet. I sounded awful, though!"

"He did at first, too," said Grandma. "I remember when he was learning to play! He sounded like a honking duck. Then he became very good. He was in a *banda* by the time he was fifteen. He played at weddings and on holidays."

"What did you do?" asked Manny.

"I learned folk dancing," said Grandma with a smile. "I learned dances that had been danced in Mexico for hundreds of years. I loved my costume! It was a dress covered with lace and ribbons."

Mama came into the room. "Look, Manny," she said. Mama showed Manny a photograph. It was Grandma when she was a young girl. Grandma was wearing the dress she had described.

"Oh, my!" said Grandma. "Can you believe that was me?"

"I can," said Manny. "You're beautiful! Were there really dances that were hundreds of years old?"

"Of course," said Grandma. "Mexico has a long history. We will go to the museum in the city one day. I will show you statues and art that are thousands of years old. The Mexican people had a fine culture. Did you know there are pyramids in Mexico?"

"No, I did not know that!" said Manny. "Are there really pyramids like the ones in Egypt?"

"That is right," said Grandma. "I climbed one when I was a young girl. I was so high up in the air! I looked down at the world below. The colors were bright like a Diego Rivera painting."

"Who is that?" asked Manny.

"Diego Rivera was one of Mexico's great painters," said Grandma. "Many everyday Mexicans created lovely folk art, too. Do you remember the dragon that I have in my house?"

"Yes," said Manny. "I love that dragon."

"That's an *alebrije*, which is a kind of Mexican folk art," said Grandma. "I brought it with me from Mexico."

"When did you come here?" asked Manny.

"I came when I was eighteen years old," said Grandma. "I was given the chance to go to college in California."

"What did you miss most?" Manny asked.

"I missed the ranch," said Grandma. "I wasn't used to living in the city. I came to love it, though. I was very glad to be here!"

"I'm glad you came, Grandma," Manny said. "I'm going to have so much to tell the class. I wonder," said Manny.

"What?" asked Grandma.

"I wonder what I will say when my children ask about their cultural heritage," said Manny.

"Tell them everything I told you about Mexico," said Grandma. "Then add what you love about living here in the United States."

"Like what?" asked Manny.

"You can tell about the games you play, your favorite foods, and holidays, such as Thanksgiving and the Fourth of July," said Grandma.

"I'll certainly have a lot to tell!" said Manny.

Scaffolded Language Development

VERB TENSE Tell students that verbs have many forms, but they all stem from the main verb called the *infinitive*. Model for students how to convert a verb from various tenses to the infinitive, using the following examples of verbs from the book: *Ms. Richards wants* (to want); *he explained* (to explain). Then read the sentences below. Have students chorally identify the verb and put it in the infinitive.

1. We walked home slowly.
2. My little sister danced to the brass band.
3. I hurried over to my grandmother.
4. The band played all night long.
5. I learned how to dance.

 **Art**

Share Your Culture Have students divide a sheet of paper into four parts. In each part, have them draw a picture of something that represents their culture. It could be a food or an item of clothing. It might be a piece of artwork or a musical instrument. Then have students label each of their pictures.

School-Home Connection

Family Heritage Ask students to talk about cultural heritage with a family member and to identify things that make up their family's culture.

Word Count: 960